Emma Elephant

A story about Proverbs

Written and illustrated by
Zoe Carter

Copyright 2017

The Bible is a great big library. Sixty-six
books in all. Some are big and some are small.

Books about the past, books about the future, letters, poems, stories that are true. And all the books are from God to you.

Let's have a look at the book of Proverbs.

'I don't understand', said Little Owl.

'Sometimes the best way to understand a difficult
idea is to tell a good story...'

At last it was the end of the school day. Emma elephant tooted with delight. Now she could go home and play.

'Don't forget to bring your homework tomorrow',
said the teacher, Mrs Bear.

Emma slumped into her seat in disappointment. She had forgotten all about it. She needed to finish it tonight after school.

Emma sulked all the way home. 'It's so unfair', she said to herself. 'I wish I didn't have to stay in and do my homework.'

'Then don't do it', said a voice from the tree.

Emma held up a magnifying glass and saw a spider. 'I am a lying spider. I will give you any lie you want. All I ask in return is that you let me wrap you in a tiny bit of my web.'

'Deal!' said Emma, 'A tiny bit of web can't hurt me.'
The lying spider hopped onto Emma's shoulder, and
they set off home.

'Welcome home, Emma', said Mummy elephant.
'What homework has Mrs Bear given you to do
tonight?' she asked.

The lying spider whispered into Emma's ear.
'Mrs Bear didn't give me any homework tonight',
she answered Mummy elephant.

Mummy elephant looked at Emma suspiciously.
'Well, we shall see what happens at school
tomorrow', she said with a frown.

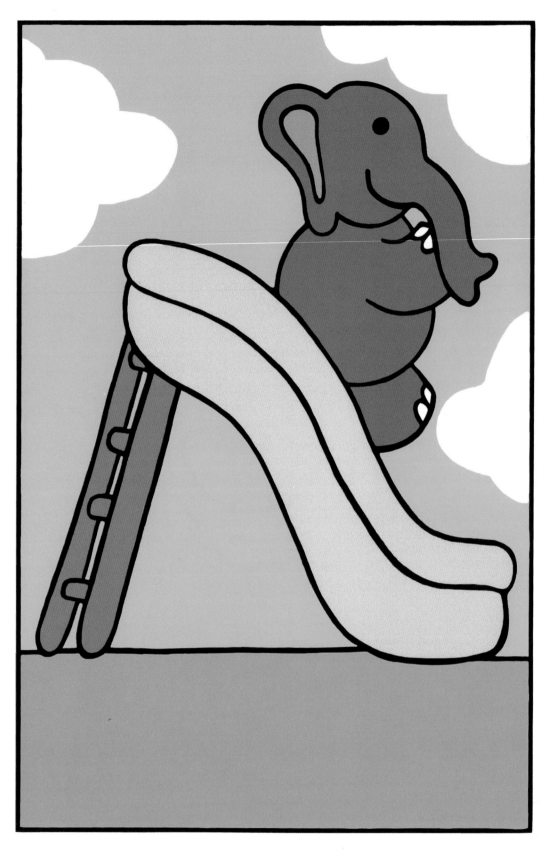

Emma went to the park and played all evening.

The next day at school, Mrs Bear asked Emma for her homework.

The lying spider gave Emma another lie.

'I couldn't do my homework because we had to go to hospital last night', she said to Mrs Bear. 'My Mummy's trunk turned orange so we had to see a doctor.'

Mrs Bear looked suspiciously at Emma.
'Well, it is the end of the day, so I think we shall
take a visit to the doctor', said Mrs Bear firmly.

Emma elephant panicked. 'Well, her trunk got better very quickly so we went home.'

'Well, I am very interested to hear the doctor tell me all about this mysterious illness', answered Mrs Bear. 'Hurry up and let's go.'

'Hello Doctor Monkey', said Mrs Bear.
'Emma tells me her Mummy came in last
night because her trunk turned orange.'

'Mummy elephant did not come in last
night, said Doctor Monkey gravely. 'And I
have never heard of anyone's trunk turning
orange.'

Emma's eyes widened in fear. 'Well, you see, we walked to the hospital, but then her trunk turned back to grey before we walked through the door, so we went back home', she blurted out

Doctor Monkey looked at Emma suspiciously.

'Well, my shift has just finished', he said. 'I think we had better visit your Mummy at home so that we can check her trunk is alright.'

Mrs Bear and Doctor Monkey marched home, with
Emma dawdling behind.

'Hello Mummy elephant', said Mrs Bear. 'Emma tells me
she did not do her homework because you went to
hospital because of an orange trunk.' Mummy elephant
frowned. 'I had no such thing', she replied sternly.

Emma was well and truly stuck. All those lies had caught her in a web.

'I knew it', said Mummy elephant. You have been talking to the lying spider. You must tell the truth or you will never be free.'

'I'm sorry I didn't do my homework, and I'm sorry I lied to you', said Emma. As she told the truth a rush of air shot out from her trunk. The lying spider and all of his cobwebs blew away.

'I forgive you, Emma', said Mummy. Never lie again. You will only get caught in a web. Always tell the truth.'

Zoe Carter lives in Edinburgh, the capital of Scotland. She loves to make puppets, drink tea with her friends, and dress up in fancy dress costumes. Her favourite animal is an octopus.

www.zoecraftbook.com

Check out Zoe's Bible craft activity website www.zoecraftbook.com
More than 100 craft activities with full step by step photographic
instructions and templates. Fun, high quality and easy. Suitable for boys
and girls. Ideal for Sunday school, church, holiday clubs, homeschooling,
family time, VBS, camps, away days and many more.

Printed in Great Britain
by Amazon